INSIGHT

Premarriage and Marriage Awareness

DR. AL HIBBERT LCPC

WESTBOW
PRESS®
A DIVISION OF THOMAS NELSON
& ZONDERVAN

WestBow Press books may be ordered through booksellers or by contacting:

WestBow Press
A Division of Thomas Nelson & Zondervan
1663 Liberty Drive
Bloomington, IN 47403
www.westbowpress.com
844-714-3454

Scripture marked KJV are taken from the Holy Bible, King James Version (Authorized Version). First published in 1611. Quoted from the KJV Classic Reference Bible, Copyright © 1983 by The Zondervan Corporation.

Scripture quotations marked (NASB) taken from the New American Standard Bible® (NASB), Copyright © 1960, 1962, 1963, 1968, 1971, 1972, 1973, 1975, 1977, 1995 by The Lockman Foundation Used by permission. www.Lockman.org

ISBN: 978-1-6642-9726-5 (sc)
ISBN: 978-1-6642-9728-9 (hc)
ISBN: 978-1-6642-9727-2 (e)

Library of Congress Control Number: 2023906405

Print information available on the last page.

WestBow Press rev. date: 04/06/2023

CONTENTS

PREFACE

During my decades in ministry and working in the area of mental health, God has always instilled in me a concern for strengthening marriages. I have seen the impact of divorce on spouses and innocent children. One of my greatest passions is to see marriages with happy endings.

This self-help book shares exactly what the title indicates—*insight.* It is based on sound biblical doctrine and principles concerning marriage and proper Christian relationships. My intent is to provide solutions for difficult challenges and to show the importance of understanding, commitment, and communication and what you should do before you say, "I do."

The five temperaments, listed later, give brief insight into how people with various personality types relate to one another. They uncover possible pitfalls or obstacles that may occur between people with different personalities.

Single life should <u>not be</u> boring; rather, it should be <u>enjoyed and celebrated</u>.

I have candidly addressed and given insight regarding premarriage and marriage awareness by providing coping strategies to live successfully and feel fulfilled.

This self-help resource is for everyone, including pastors, counselors, and those who are interested in finding ways to deal with the transition from single life to marriage.

—Dr. Al Hibbert

Trust is the glue of life.

⇩

It's the most essential ingredient
in **effective communication**.

⇩

It's the foundational principle
that holds all relationships.

—Stephen Covey

ACKNOWLEDGMENTS

All my gratitude goes to God, who has sustained me, carried me, and cared for me for over seventy years. He has always showed up when I needed him most—in the valley, on the plains, and on the mountain. Words can hardly express my heartfelt gratitude to God.

My thanks to my wife of over fifty years, Iona, who has been a strong support to me through thick and thin. She has been my eyes and ears in getting this book to make sense.

My thanks also go to my three sons, Chris, Dwane, and Craig; my grandchildren, Dwane Jr., Demia, and Maverick; my in-laws, Marlisa and Linnet; my bro, Ed; and my sisters, nieces, and nephews. Together, we say thanks to God for rescuing my son Dwane from the cold claws of death. He survived COVID-19 after a long struggle.

Thanks to all my friends and supporters who have poured into my life during the ins and outs of my many years of ministry.

To the Arnos and all the staff of the NCCA, who have invested and poured into my life to make me who I am today

To the Ellis Institute and its founder, the late Albert Ellis, in the training of Rational Emotive Behavior Therapy (REBT).

To all my past students, who I helped fulfill their counseling goals.

To all my clients—in their eyes, I helped them, but they also helped me because this book is a result of the experiences gained in the counseling office.

To my new family at WestBow Publishing.

To my good friend Ikolyn Barrimond. I cannot thank her enough for helping me with this project. She has willingly put the final touch on this work.

To all my readers, may this book be a lamp to your feet and a light to your path in your time of making decisions, even the difficult ones.

You are as strong as the
test you overcome.

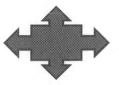

Be careful of what goes out of your
mouth gate. You cannot call it back.

Ignore the flaws of the
imperfect because no one is
perfect, not even you.

Effective unity produces
effective results.

INTRODUCTION

Choose to think healthy thoughts, and you will develop a clearer outlook of yourself, and others. You also will feel better about your unique self.

As a young man, I knew nothing about counseling. As a matter of fact, I had no premarital counseling from my pastor or anyone experienced in marriage.

When I told my pastor of my intention to get married, he pointed his finger at me and said, "Just remember that this is not *guinep* time." He meant that I should not engage in sex before I got married. In his mind, if one refrained from sex before marriage, one was good to go. That was our five-minute counseling session. I even was advised to stay away from my fiancée. Just imagine—no dating, no getting to know the person with whom I would spend the rest of my life.

A relationship is much more than sex. Later on, I'll give you a glimpse of climbing the stairs from dating to marriage.

I thank God for my father, who was a good role model. By watching him, I learned that a successful marriage requires a triad (three), not just a dyad (two). My father was a police constable, substitute pastor, shoemaker, farmer, and much more. He was a very good example to us children. He was not a trained counselor, but the entire community always looked to him for guidance. Interestingly, it seems that they always left his presence better than they came.

As I grew older, before I had any formal training, people would ask for my help during times of marital conflict. Today,

I am an authority on the subject of marriage and family counseling. I have helped hundreds of hurting individuals find the strength to resolve conflicts in marriage and family. I also have trained many in the field of counseling.

This book will give insight and shed some light as you think about your wholeness as a couple or a single person.

If you have a singleness of mind, you will be better able to accept your unique self. *Singleness of mind* means you do not live a life of fantasy, imagination, past relationships, or guilt. If you are married, healthy thinking will help you accept yourself and respect the sacredness of marriage, as it is a lifetime commitment. If you are single, healthy thinking will give you the tenacity to maintain godly principles as you strive to be a person of excellence.

Avoid unhealthy negative thinking. Many people who fail in their relationships blame it on impulse because they did not stop long enough to consider the consequences of unhealthy choices.

Webster's Dictionary defines the word *impulse* as follows:

> a sudden or impelling force; a state of mind or impelling stimulus; a sudden inclination to act

You were given the ability to control your thinking and to monitor your pulse rate during hormonal changes in the body. Medication or supplements will not do everything for you. There are some things you must do for yourself, like "Casting down imaginations and taking every thought captive" (2 Corinthians 10:5). Remember that the battle is in your mind.

The "real you" is unseen. You live inside a shell called a body. It's OK to admire a person's body, but that is like admiring a beautiful house and not knowing who lives inside. To fully accept what you see on the outside, you must get on the inside. This is where counseling comes in. Acceptance must be based on character and reputation. Character highlights an individual's qualities and traits.

Please note that someone can have a reputation as a great sportsman but possess a flawed character.

Apart from character and reputation, we all were born with an inborn temperament by which we are affected.

CHAPTER 1

Why Relationships Are in Trouble Today

FAILURE TO KNOW ONESELF BEFORE sharing oneself with someone else leads to relationship trouble. Find yourself before you find a mate.

Here are three reasons why people will refuse to follow you:

1. You have no self-confidence.
2. You do not know who you are.
3. You do not know where you are going.

Why does a male struggle to be a man?

Being born male does not make someone a responsible man. He had no choice when he was born naturally as a male, but he has a choice whether to responsibly develop his manhood, and I am not talking about sex.

Genesis 1:27 says that God created male and female. Genesis 1:31 says that God called it very good. The only perfect marriages are those that can identify with Genesis 1 and 2. After Genesis 2, when man sinned, he was broken and needed much work.

Effects of the Past

In the past, men operated on the premise that they were in charge of the family, and they were respected by their wives. Regardless of what they did for a living, they were respected in the home. Unlike today, wives did not have to tell their husbands to "be a man." Husbands knew their places, and so did their wives.

> ➤ The man bought the house; the wife took care of the house.
> ➤ He brought home the money; she spent the money.
> ➤ He brought home the meat; she prepared the meat.
> ➤ He gave her a seed; she nurtured the seed.

The woman's job was to meet the man's needs. She cleaned the house, prepared meals, cleaned his clothes, and fulfilled his sexual needs.

Although in the past, couples might have loved each other, marriages did not merely function on love. A marriage was both wife and husband partnering together. All they had to do for a successful marriage was to perform their roles well.

During the Silent Generation (1925–1945), a massive change occurred. World War II took place from 1939 to 1945. This greatly affected the family because the roles were reversed, and this affects us to this day.

After the men were sent off to war, their absence created a shortage of workers. The jobs that the men had performed had to be done by women because the factories had to keep producing. The women made and supplied the bullets while the men fired them. After the war, some men did not make it back. Some came back without limbs. Those who made it back were now without jobs because in their absence the women were forced to assume men's roles so they could survive.

For five long years, women had been in charge of the homes, playing the roles of father and mother. Many of the men who returned tried to fit in because the roles had been reversed, and the men did not feel like men anymore. The family was greatly affected; everything that made a man feel like a man was gone. All he had left was his physical strength, which he would use, at times, for abuse to express his manhood.

Women had their own houses, drove their own cars, and had their own bank accounts. They were now living in a state of independence, no longer depending on men to provide.

In 1949, Simone de Beauvoir introduced women's liberation in her book *The Second Sex*. The feminist movement had a major impact on where we are today.

Implications

Women rarely depend on men to be providers, recognize them as the head of the home, or need them for protection. Many women now carry guns in their purses. The only thing many women depend on a man for is meeting sexual needs. Most marriages today are barely surviving because the women are in charge and now tell the men to "man up." Those words sometimes lead to emotional, physical, spousal, or child abuse, as well as separation or divorce.

Today's women, although independent, require much more than their mothers or grandmothers, who simply played their roles without requiring much. Men now find it difficult to meet women's needs. They may only think of the values of their ancestors, but they cannot instill them. The difference is that men were in charge then, but now, they are not.

> ➤ Today, a woman's number-one need is affection. Women are emotional thinkers. They make many decisions based on emotions. Women think with their hearts.
> ➤ A man's number-one need is sex. Men are logical thinkers who are not easily affected by emotions. Men evaluate conditions, and they reason through important decisions. Men think with their brains.

Most of our foreparents stayed married because the marriage functioned through roles, and husbands and wives were accountable to each other. Today, many men are incarcerated, and women are single. The divorce rate is climbing in the church and in the world. One of the reasons is men's inability to "man up."

The Pharisees ask Jesus a question: Did Moses command that a man give his wife a letter of divorce and send her away? Jesus replied, "Moses permitted you to divorce your wives because your hearts were hard. *But it was not this way from the beginning*" (Matthew 19:8, emphasis added). Jesus was talking about perfection in Genesis 1 and humankind's brokenness after chapter 2.

Under Mosaic Law, the man was in charge; only he could divorce his wife. Today, a wife can divorce her husband. Divorce hurts.

In Malachi 2:16, God says he hates divorce because it is full of violence; that is, it is cruel and wrong.

Divorce Is Death without a Burial

Between 1867 and 1879, the divorce rate in America was only .03 percent. Today, according to a study from Baylor University, "Despite *Evangelical Christians* strong pro-family values, they have higher divorce rates" (emphasis added). Many pastors are living with their second or third wives, not to mention the members. Divorce is a death worse than physical death. When individuals die a physical death, we bury them, and eventually, the memories may fade away. When a marriage dies, there is no burial; instead, you keep bumping into the live corpse in the grocery store, at the mall, at work, and so on.

Divorce can be a painful experience.

> ➢ An old proverb says, "A loose dog never understands what a tied dog is going through."
> ➢ You are not ready for marriage because you feel horny; that's not a reason to get married.
> ➢ You are not ready to be married if you need to be married; your need will only drain your spouse.
> ➢ You are not ready if you are not fully developed. Seek to be developed before marriage.
> ➢ You are not ready if you are living in brokenness. Marriage requires wholeness of body, soul, and spirit.
> ➢ You are not ready if you think your time is running out. If you are in right standing with God, that thought will never cross your mind.
> ➢ You are not ready until you are ready spiritually, logically, and emotionally.
> ➢ You are not ready because you need a family.

> ➤ You are not ready just because your friends are married.
> ➤ You are not ready because you are not happy.
> ➤ You are not ready because of a prophecy you received.
> ➤ You are not ready because you're having problems (e.g., no place to live).
> ➤ You are not ready if you are tired of being physically single.
> ➤ Readiness starts with singleness of heart. You must first seek to be spiritually single.

Four Reasons Why Couples Divorce

1. They want to escape a painful, loveless relationship without giving themselves time to heal from emotional scars.

   Suddenly, the old scab of the last relationship comes off, and it's déjà vu. They move into new relationships too fast, and before long, they experience the same problems from which they ran.

2. One or both seek satisfaction with someone else who, in their eyes, seems to be a better fit.

   In many cases, the anticipated goal is never experienced, and the comparison syndrome kicks in, because everyone's talents and gifts vary. The age-old saying is, "You can't have your cake and eat it." The grass only looked greener when they first saw it; then the season changed.

3. One party gets tired of the irresponsible actions of the other. Such acts may come in different shapes and sizes,

like money, sex, family interference, immaturity, culture, status, and so forth.

4. They find it hard to commit to a relationship of broken trust.

A Tale of the Pear and Its Four Seasons

There was once a man who had four sons. He wanted to teach his sons not to judge too fast and not to give up easily. He sent each one of the boys on their way to the same pear tree that was far from their village.

The first son went in the winter, the second went in the spring, the third went in the summer, and the youngest son went in the autumn. When everyone had visited the tree and returned, the father gathered them and asked them to describe what they had seen.

The first son said the tree was ugly, bent, and distorted.

The second son said that it was not possible that he had seen the same tree; the tree he had found was covered with green buds and a promise of fertility.

The third son said his brothers had not seen the same tree that he saw. His tree had radiant pear blossoms that spread a sweet scent, and it seemed to him to be the most beautiful tree he had ever seen.

The youngest son said he saw a totally different tree, one that was full of fruit, a symbol of a complete life and satisfaction.

The father listened to his sons' stories and told them that each of them was right. They all had seen the same tree, but each had visited the pear tree during a different season. That was the lesson that he wanted to convey to them—one cannot judge trees or people for one season. Their true nature, as well as the joy and love they bring, was a result we can see only at the end of the year, when all the seasons have passed.

If you decide to opt out in the winter, you will miss the promise of a new life that comes with spring; the beauty and warmth of the summer; and the abundance of autumn. Do not let the pain and difficulty of a season of your life destroy your long-term happiness.

I often hear my clients say, "I'm tired." The irresponsible actions of a spouse can create major roadblocks for the other, such as to do with money, sexual violation, allowing family interference, immaturity, culture, and status. Saying they are *tired* indicates they're ready to quit.

From my perspective, the implications of divorce can bring joy or sorrow. Some divorces leave individuals in a state of regret. In extreme cases, some couples are better off terminating the relationship than trying to fix it, but that should never be the first option.

Divorce should be the result of ongoing abuse or sexual immorality, not because two people find it hard to communicate or one person is a nag. If both parties are willing to recover what they lost, a resolution is imminent.

Here is a secret: The only way to fix a struggling marriage is to divorce the old marriage and start over with the *same spouse*. During my years in the counseling office using therapeutic methods, I saw dead marriages live again.

It's been some years, but I can remember a particular couple who came close to being physical in my office. They were both cursing at each other, and for a while, they seemed to forget where they were and why they'd come. I did not try to stop them. I wanted them to unload, and they did, as I watched and listened. After the blowup, they both apologized, and we continued the session. After ten sessions with them, the blinders came off. They divorced the old marriage and started a new one.

I have seen marriages in trouble based on one's childhood experiences, but many problems are a result of learned behavior. Sometimes during counseling, we are tempted to stop and focus on exposing childhood problems; that approach is good and bad. We must only open doors that we are able to close. Explaining a problem does not necessarily solve it. The solution lies in understanding why individuals do what they do. Unmasking the problem is just the tip of the iceberg. Rational emotive behavioral therapy (REBT) uses the ABC model to explain the interaction between thoughts, emotions, and behaviors. There are many types of psychoanalytic approaches, like transactional analysis, Gestalt therapy, and more that explore an individual's personality and how it has shaped the individual experience, particularly from one's childhood. I find that using the Arno Profile System (APS) provides an x-ray view of why individuals get to where they are.

Perhaps you have thought of getting a divorce, which many couples desire from time to time; you or your spouse might be giving it serious thought. You might have taken some steps toward it, but you are still searching for answers by reading books and asking questions. That tells me you are not sure you want to follow through. It's never too late to change your mind about carrying out a divorce.

A little bit of hope can open the door to a new level of communication. This cannot work if only one party wants it or is waiting for the other person to change. It requires both minds to be open to another try.

Although divorce was meant to solve a problem, in many cases, it doesn't. Many problems, however, can be fixed. Try before you quit.

> But seek ye first the kingdom of God, and his righteousness; and all these things shall be added unto you.
>
> —Matthew 6:33 (KJV)

CHAPTER 2

Understanding: The Key to Soundness in a Relationship

LIFE IS LIKE A LADDER. As you climb, you realize there is a lesson in every step. From birth, you are affected by millions of different personalities and behaviors while climbing.

This is not a book on temperament, but it does offer a brief snapshot of why relationships experience unseen complexities. Everyone falls somewhere within the five temperaments:

1. Melancholy
2. Sanguine
3. Supine
4. Choleric
5. Phlegmatic

Early scientific discoveries reported only four temperaments. In 1983, however, Drs. Richard and Phyllis Arno of the National Christian Counselors Association (of which I am a member) made the phenomenal discovery of a fifth temperament, the supine, which was not mentioned in the writings of previous temperament researchers:

1. Hippocrates, 460–370 BC
2. Empedocles, 495–435 BC
3. Galen, AD 131–200
4. Maimonides, 1135–1204
5. Nicholas Culpepper, 1616–1634
6. Immanuel Kant, 1724–1804
7. Alfred Adler, 1879–1937
8. Ivan Pavlov, 1849–1936
9. Hans J. Eysenck, 1916
10. Tim LaHaye, 1926

The Gender Difference

> We have the responsibility of living up to our potential and correcting all correctable defects. Our self-worth as well as our Christian witness will benefit from praising God for designing us the way we are. (Arno 1998)

Apart from their inborn temperament, men and women are opposites in every way. We are all different.

People are different because of how they were born and raised. They are affected by the following:

- Temperament
- Personality
- Environmental effects
- Cultures
- Race and ethnicity

People act differently because of emotional effects:

- Past experiences
- Past hurts
- Past failures

These things play a major role in our lives. People allow their past to dominate their present; thus, it filters into their future because they close the doors to knowledge.

People are different because of gender.

Men	**Women**
Are driven by sight	Are driven by emotions
Are less committed	Are more committed
Forget little things	Remember little things
Are more romantic	Are more loving
Find it hard to admit fears	Find it easy to admit fears
Have wandering minds	Are more settled

> Understanding and communication
> are the keys to opening closed
> relationship doors.

CHAPTER 3

Four Stages of Before and After Marriage

1. Romance
2. Reality
3. Dissolution
4. Reconstruction

Dealing with *After* when *Before* Is Gone

MARRIAGE WAS INTENTIONAL. GOD DID not intend for marriage to be two but one. In Genesis 1:27, God created man. The words *create* originates from the Hebrew word *bara*, which means "made from nothing." He then put the entire human race in one man.

Genesis 2:7 states that God made man. The word *made* originates from the Hebrew word *asa*, which means "form or made from something already created." The Hebrew word *ish* means man.

God put the man to sleep, went into him, took out a rib, and fashioned it. Then he woke up the man and presented his "rib" to him. The man must have said, "Wow! this came out of me? I'll call her woman." God created the entire human race of male and female but only made one man. The woman was an extension of the man. The man called her wo-man because she came out of him.

> And the LORD God fashioned into a woman the rib which He had taken from the man and brought her to the man. (Genesis 2:22 NASB)

Genesis 2:24 narrates the close relationship between man and woman's sexual union: "Therefore a man leaves his father and his mother and cling to his wife." It's a kingly relationship. "And they shall be one flesh."

Expectation in a relationship causes pressure. That's why the saloons are always full. Women spend appalling amounts of money to prevent the broken man from looking elsewhere.

Couples will make statements like, "I never expected things would get to this." That's a flawed expectation that leads to disappointment, and that leads to separation.

> Love one another because love is of God. (1 John 4:7)

God is the very essence of true love. When God says *I love you*, it's *agape* love. That's real love with no conditions. Because God is love, agape is the only glue that will hold a marriage together.

Some relationships are held by *philia* love. That's a friendship based on expectation. *Eros* love is almost like a barter system— treat me good; I'll treat you good. When you genuinely love, you can genuinely care.

Some relationships are based on *storge* love; that is mere fondness or familiarity. A couple may be bonded together through parents or family members. Except for agape, all others—philia, eros, and storge—are based on conditions. Those types of love are good but will not survive storms.

In 1 Peter 5:7, God said that he cares for you. When you care, you don't have any problems meeting a need. God cares for us so much that he made provisions for us before the foundation of the world. God hates divorce because it causes dysfunction. Children have to live in two homes, one week with Daddy and one week with Mommy. Divorce has grave psychological effects.

Marital Types and Behaviors

Each marriage will fall into one of the categories listed below:

1. Power
   ➢ Who is in charge of what and when?
   ➢ Intimacy between the dyad and subsystems
   ➢ Inclusion/exclusion; from whom do we triangulate?
2. Marital Classification (Christian psychology, Minirth and Meier)
   ➢ Conflict habituated—held together by fear of loneliness
   ➢ Deviated marriage—held together by children; high conflict; no zest
   ➢ Passive congenial—pleasant but no intimacy
   ➢ Vital marriage—one major area of common interest
   ➢ Total marriage—most interests, activities, and goals pursued in common

Types of Marital Counseling

❖ Individual—one person sees a counselor.

❖ Joint—husband and wife see the same counselor.

❖ Collaborative—husband and wife see different counselors.

❖ Concurrent—husband and wife see the same counselor at separate times.

Different Stages of Marriage

• Romance

A couple comes together in marriage after the wedding bliss. There is so much excitement on the wedding day. Everyone joins in the grand celebration of this couple who extended an invitation. There are gifts, fun and laughter, hugs and kisses, toasts, cake, wine, food, photographs, flowers, dancing, and tossing the bouquet.

Then comes the time of driving off into the sunset to the honeymoon. Everyone and everything has been blocked out for this special memory. The couple is full of strong positive feelings, The couple totally accept each other and feel surrounded by an almost unbreakable warmth.

• **Reality**

This is when the glow subsides. Each begins to see the other person's faults. They become critical of each other and see most things through a negative eye. This new discovery unveils weaknesses and problems with the other partner. Individuals become blinded to their own faults and weaknesses and begin the blame game. This forms a dividing barrier that brings a feeling of coldness that hardens into resentment. This causes the couple to give up, which, in effect, causes them to establish separate lives. At this point, one of two things will happen:

1. **Dissolution.** The couple accepts that the marriage is over and gets a divorce.
2. **Reconstruction.** The couple agrees to get help and begin the reconstruction process.

A very important question is, why did this happen? You can love God with all your heart and still get divorced. You can love your spouse and still get divorced because love is not what holds a marriage together.

One of the big mistakes people make is getting carried away with "I love you" and not asking the most important question: *Why do you love me?* Marriages fail because most love is based on *conditions*, and whenever there is a reason, there is also a condition. When you say I love you, you're saying that I love you just the way you are now. Real love is not through one's eye gate; it's through the heart gate.

Every couple cherishes the three magic words "I love you." One partner uses those words to kick-start emotions in the other person, but this should never be so. Here is the danger: if the husband, for example, changes from who he is, the wife might not love him anymore, and vice versa. When he says he loves her because of her beauty or shape, or she says she loves him because he has a good job or a great house, and later, those things change, the love also will change.

Let's face it; nothing stays the same forever. Things and people will change. The teeth might decay, the breath might smell, or the hair might fall out. The snoring, the chronic cough, or sickness might change their life together in a flash.

People have the great expectation that things will get better. Thus, they do not like the phrase in the marital vows that says "for better and for worse, for richer, for poorer." If life takes a downward turn, they fall apart. The "worse" could be a test to see where you stand, so don't be too hasty to reject it. "Better" might be wrapped up in worse. Faithfulness requires consistency. Divorce is not a part of a godly marriage. It has grave psychological effects, mainly on the children.

Satan infused disunity that caused dysfunction in the first family God created. Genesis 3:12–13 tells us that the man blamed Eve and defended himself to God by saying, "The woman you gave me, she did this."

It's better not to vow (Ecclesiastes 5:5).

"Thy vows are upon me" until death (Psalm 56:12).

In marriage, you make a promise to your spouse, and you vow to God, who judges.

Kingdom marriage means being totally committed to fulfilling the other's needs. Keeping an agreement requires a sense of accountability and integrity within oneself.

CHAPTER 4

Keep a Level Head

COMMITMENT AND DEDICATION INSTILL TRUST.

A broken agreement destroys trust. It affects communication and erodes intimacy.

> Therefore, my beloved brethren, be ye steadfast, unmoveable, always abounding ... forasmuch as ye know that your labor is not in vain ... (1 Corinthians 15:58)

There are those who are curious about achieving. There are those who are focused. There are those who plan. There are those who only dream. There are those who talk about it. There are those who just criticize. There are those who look forward to it. There are those who only wish. There are those who watch. Then there are those who are totally committed to getting things done.

> Commitment is the cornerstone of creative change.

> —Michael Gelb

Consider the following:

> ➤ The quality of a person's life is in direct proportion to his or her commitment; he or she demonstrates that commitment every moment with his or her thoughts and actions.
> ➤ The difference between excellence and mediocrity is commitment.
> ➤ The path that runs from the dream to the achievement is paved with commitment all the way.
> ➤ Those who make the commitment—those who give their dreams the power of focus—are those who will realize their dreams.
> ➤ No matter how worthy, admirable, or fiercely desired the goal may be, it takes commitment and action to make it a reality.
> ➤ If you're curious, if you're focused, and if you're thinking and dreaming and planning, take that powerful step up to being committed. Make your hopes and dreams count for something. Be committed.
> ➤ Don't panic over disagreements. Agree to disagree.
> ➤ Healthy disagreement can lead to stronger resolutions about making a decision.

As important as love is in the marriage, it is not what keeps the marriage together through the storms. Storms are inevitable, but the pledge one makes to withstand the storms is called *commitment*.

CHAPTER 5

The Need Factor

THE GREATEST ENEMY BETWEEN A man and a woman in marriage is the refusal to meet a need. Everyone has needs. There are five needs that drive us. These needs are built into our genetic structure—just as much a part of our genetic heritage as our arms and legs. We must learn to live the best way we can to satisfy the need for love, relationship, acceptance, involvement, and praise.

The enemies to these needs are the following:

Anger	Malice	Spite
Bitterness	Pain	Stress
Blame	Rebellion	Stubbornness
Distrust	Rejection	Unforgiveness
Hate	Resentment	Withdrawal
Inferiority	Self-pity	
Insecurity	Shame	

Everyone has the following needs:

> ➤ *Need to reproduce.* God put this need in man. Every man wants to see fruit after seeds are sown.
> ➤ *Need to belong.* We need to love and be loved; we need association and socialization.

➢ *Need for power and control.* There's an inner need for dominance and to survive. There's a need to act. The drive for power may conflict with the need to belong.

➢ *Need for freedom.* It is so important for us to know God in a personal way. If we cannot connect with our needs in a godly way, it creates an opening for evil.

➢ *Need for fun.* Life was meant to be enjoyed, but we are not to be consumed by pleasure alone.

Two valuable yet toxic issues in marriage are money and sex.

In the dichotomy of marriage, two imperfect people searching for meaning or balance always will experience conflict.

Our basic needs still drive us, and we must learn to live the best way we can to satisfy those needs without displeasing God. Our fleshly bodies must be controlled by the Holy Spirit, but there are certain needs the Holy Spirit will not satisfy. When your spouse indicates his or her need for sex, never deprive him or her unless there is a valid reason.

When the need is there, he or she is like a car with a warning light that indicates it needs gas. Refusal to heed that signal can result in great danger. Disobeying that law may cost you the car you claim to love dearly. When the signal is on, you don't pour water or some other liquid in the tank; it must be gas.

> When your spouse needs sex, it's not time to speak in tongues, pray, or call on the name of Jesus.

The car will continue running after you pull off the road and gas up.

For many men who are denied, this is what happens: a fight. Why? A need was not met. Request number two; need not met; fight again. By the third refusal, the man loses his appetite, feelings, and interest in a wife he loves. He is now beginning to think of another gas station.

Men, remember that women need affection more than sex. You don't just toss gas in the car. You use care to make sure it goes in the tank. It's never a good thing when you are satisfied, but she is frustrated. Men, if you don't provide, don't make demands. Men, love your wives.

Women, it's not how well you cook or how good you are in bed. One of men's greatest needs is respect. While you expect love, show and give much respect to your spouse and speak highly of him.

CHAPTER 6

The Misconception of Singleness

SINGLENESS, IN GOD'S EYES, IS to be separate, unique, original, whole, and complete.

> ➤ In the beginning, God gave all instructions to a single man.
> ➤ God began the entire human race with a single man.
> ➤ Except for the animals, man was all alone in the garden.

The Hebrew definition of *alone* is *all one*. Adam saw himself as being alone because God did not tell him that he was carrying the entire human race inside of him. In Adam's eyes, he was alone—but he wasn't.

> Remember the former things, those of long ago;
> I am God, and there is no other; I am God, and
> there is none like me. I make known the end from
> the beginning, from ancient times, what is still to
> come. I say, My purpose will stand, and I will do
> all that I please. (Isaiah 46:9–10)

God created endings before beginnings. That means he created the entire human race first; then he created man and placed us all in him. Then he made a house (body) and placed us all in it.

Then God looked at the body (alone, all one) and said it was not good for man to carry the entire human race and still be alone. The man had no clue that he was carrying the end of all things; his job was to develop what God had finished.

We are all affected by one man's error (Romans 5:12). When Adam sinned, everything he was carrying became "all have sinned." We could say that God did not give him a literal house with furniture, but think about it—God gave him trees and hid the house and furniture in the trees. Again, he created the ending before beginning.

It is OK to be single. On many occasions during counseling sessions, young single women have asked me, "Do you think I'm attractive?"

I always have responded, "Why?"

This question always received many different responses. It seemed that their common ambition was to be married and have children. That, of course, is a good desire, but what if you were never married and never had children? That does not make you any less a woman. It is OK to be single and not have children; that does not make you any less attractive. Women frequently have a self-deprecating attitude and lose sight of their uniqueness.

Keep a positive outlook with the following in mind: God wants you to love, appreciate, and accept your unique self, whether you're single or married, have children or do not have children.

When you walk in the newness of God's love and grace, it gives you the ability to lift yourself to a higher level of self-acceptance. Besides, when your negative self-perception changes, it will be easier to accept your singleness.

> ➤ Look at the intricacies of the human frame.
> ➤ "You are fearfully and wonderfully made" (Psalm 139).
> ➤ You are a precious gem.
> ➤ You are specially designed by the Master Designer.
> ➤ You are a special single person.

The psalmist could not have put it better when he said the following:

> For you did knit me together in my mother's womb. I will confess and praise you, Wonderful are Your works … my frame was not hidden from You, when I was being formed in secret, intricately, and curiously wrought (as if embroidered with various colors) … Your eyes saw my unformed substance. How precious and weighty also are your thoughts to me … If I could count them, they are more in number than the sand (Psalm 139:13–18 AMP)

You are the optimum of God's love, so enjoy being single. Make good use of every passing moment. If you keep feeling sorry for yourself by putting yourself down, you will not be able to love and care for a partner in the way that you should. You must like yourself before you can like someone else. If your single life is dull and dismal, it will carry over into your marriage. Even if you are melancholy and find it hard to crawl out of that shell, try to like yourself.

> Remember that you are "fearfully and wonderfully made," and you deserve to be happy.

Many singles have locked themselves in prisons of self-pity, or they play the blame game. Remember that being single is OK. I am aware of the loneliness of single life, but loneliness does not mean *aloneness*. If you do not appreciate and enjoy your singleness, you will make costly mistakes.

CHAPTER 7

The Church and Marriage

I HAVE SEEN MANY BELIEVERS who were excited about the Lord and his work but became discouraged because their expectations were not met. One reason for that was that they came to the church for the wrong reasons. Some got involved to satisfy their sexual needs and then left the church. I believe that when Jesus is truly Lord and Master of your life, you will experience a fulfilling, satisfying, and purposeful life.

> I beseech you therefore, brethren, by the mercies of God, that ye present your bodies a living sacrifice, holy, acceptable unto God, your reasonable service. And be not conformed to this world: but be ye transformed by the renewing of your mind, that ye may prove what is that good, and acceptable, and perfect, will of God. (Romans 12:1–2)

During my years in the counseling office, clients would say things like, "I love my wife [husband], and that is the only reason I am here. This is the last straw," or "We have already seen individual lawyers regarding divorce, but he [she] asked me to come see you, so I am here."

Why do you suppose there are so many millions of couples who separate and then, within a short time, find someone else?

More than 200,000 marriages in the United States end in divorce and remarriage before the second anniversary. Think of a young woman, only twenty-four years old, who already has been through two divorces, each relationship lasting less than one year. In my opinion, such marriages based on a contract.

Contract Marriage

Marriage in the secular world is basically a contract between a man, a woman, and the state. The two parties involved may experience temperament incompatibility and decide to discontinue the relationship. They both go their own separate ways without any spiritual consequence. It is unfortunate that many in the church have adopted this secular approach instead of the biblical approach, which is called a covenant marriage.

Covenant Marriage

Biblical marriage is a covenant between a man, a woman, and God. It is *not* a contract; it's referred to as a covenant. A covenant cannot legitimately be broken. God appeared to Abraham and promised to make him a great nation. He did so with a covenant. A covenant was God's way of saying to Abraham, "I will not renege on the promise." The kingdom marriage exists as a covenant relationship and should only be broken honorably by death or in the case of adultery. (Read Matthew 19:3–8.)

Thousands of divorces are filed every day by spouses who are trading in their spouses for new models. Marriage has become just like trading in a car. I've seen people who got carried away by the sight of a newer model and later wished they had kept the old one. Here's a good example: some years ago, one of my brothers bought a fairly new SUV. It looked immaculate inside and out, the perfect-looking, perfect-driving car. Two weeks later, however, it left him stranded on the highway and had to be towed to the dealers. The old one was still faithfully sitting in the parking lot where he'd parked it. It waited and was ready to serve him, as it always had.

Many people use the same approach in relationships, leaving one for the other. It's not because the old one doesn't work well; it's man's idea that new is always better.

I was sitting beside a young woman on a train from New York to Washington some years ago. As we talked, she asked me if I was married.

I responded, "Yes, for fifteen years."

Her eyes widened as she asked, "To the same person?" Then she said, "I'm divorced. I wish I could live with one person that long."

Her view of marriage was that it was just *living with* someone, but it's much more than that.

> Wives, be subject to your own husbands, as to the Lord. For the husband is the head of the wife, as Christ also is the head of the church, He Himself being the Savior of the body. (Ephesians 5:23–33)

Two Tragic Approaches to Commitment

I wonder if people genuinely believe what they utter from their lips. Do they believe in the real God and the real heaven and hell?

Some people make a Jesus decision based on what they hear because it sounds good, or they are scared because they've heard about the horrors of hell. They never made an honest commitment to follow Jesus.

Some decide to enter a relationship based on what they see or hear, but they never consider whether or not they are ready to make a commitment.

Remember that there is a difference between a decision and a commitment—that's clear based on most failed marriages today. Statistics show that at least half of all marriages will end in divorce. Every person who enters marriage made a decision to do so. They made a promise as they repeated their vows before a preacher, and they kissed and took their first walk as husband and wife together. There is an expectation of living happily ever after, but in a short time, some of them break up.

Marriages fail because people enter this sacred institution based on personal needs. Some marry just to save the family reputation. Such marriages begin failing long before the wedding day.

Couples separate and divorce because one or both parties made a decision but not a commitment to each other. Marriage was not designed to be used as an experiment or test run. It was designed by God for a man and woman to make a lifetime commitment to each other.

When a man and a woman understand God's intent, *commitment* will help them through whatever they encounter during the marriage. They will remember that change is inevitable.

Commitment has to do with the nuts and bolts that hold the relationship together.

Love is the fuel that keeps it going.

Love sometimes caves in during a real storm, but commitment will take you through the storm.

Paul's Plea for Commitment

The apostle Paul did not give a command; he made a plea for commitment. To commit to God means yielding completely and surrendering to him. When a true commitment is made, you don't just say you made a mistake. He said,

> I beseech you therefore, brethren ... Do not be conformed, but be transformed. (Romans 12:1–2)

The word *conformed* is an outward action that does not necessarily mean that there is inner change. The word *transformed*, from the English word *metamorphosis*, is inner change, which affects outward actions.

Jesus's words in Matthew 5 refers to inner change.

➢ We are referred to as light, and we are required to keep shining.
➢ Salt makes a difference in our conversations.

➤ As long as we are shining, we are doing everything possible to eliminate the darkness.

➤ When our conversations are well seasoned, the message we send to others says, "I am committed."

CHAPTER 8

Insiders and Outsiders: Who Are They?

INSIDERS ARE THOSE WHO ARE connected to the world system without regard for godly directions. They are citizens of the world system. *Outsiders* are the committed children of God with regard for godly directions, just passing through this world without becoming citizens of it.

> For we are strangers before thee, and sojourners, as were all our fathers: our days on the earth are as a shadow, and is none abiding. (1 Corinthians 22:15)

Paul said about himself, "Not that I have already attained or am already reached my destination; but I press" (Philippians 3:11–12). The apostle does not want us to become conformed to the world system (comfortable, as insiders) with a worldly approach to relationships but to remember that from a spiritual standpoint, we are outsiders just passing through the land.

Outsiders do not have the temporary luxury of the insiders. Godly couples are being watched by the world. Even in their silence, they have high expectations of us. As called-out children of God, we will have to struggle harder to survive in the world system because it was not designed for our survival. As outsiders, we are required to work harder at everything we do and are involved in. Outsiders must express a higher level of commitment to succeed on the job, in the home, and in their marriages because the world knows that Christians work by standards.

Jesus said, "let your light shine before others, that they may see."
Matthew 5:16 (NIV)

Christ equates marriage to the church. As the church is subject to Christ, so also the wives ought to be to their husbands. Husbands, love your wives, just as Christ also loved the church and gave himself up for her, so that he might sanctify her, having cleansed her by the washing of water with the Word. That he might present to himself the church in all her glory, having no spot or wrinkle or any such thing but that she would be holy and blameless.

Husbands ought also to love their wives as their own bodies. He who loves his own wife loves himself, for no one ever hated his own flesh but nourishes and cherishes it, just as Christ also does the church because we are members of his body.

CHAPTER 9

The Absence of Godly Men

THERE IS A VACUUM IN the family today due to the absence of godly men. There is almost nothing as bad as a father abandoning his responsibility for his children. A man's duty as priest and king is first, to train up the child, and second, to bring the best out of his wife by helping to build her self-esteem and self-worth. Such requires work, which is the second thing God gave man before he gave him a woman. The first thing he gave man was the opportunity to dwell in his presence. Unfortunately, that space is left unoccupied—if only man could get back in the presence of the Lord.

- ❖ A man is to love his own wife even as himself, and the wife must see to it that she respects her husband.
- ❖ Women are more committed to godly affairs than men. Places of worship are not short of women; they are the backbone of the church.
- ❖ There are many empty pews waiting for the men to take up their rightful place as leaders.
- ❖ Men are in short supply in the church because of a lack of commitment to God and family. We call for men to get back in the presence of God and bring completion to women.

A Comparison of the Church and a Marriage

Commitment to the church means deciding on a place of worship together and moving in for a permanent stay. When a wife and husband make a commitment to God that they will willingly use their talents and gifts to serve, it becomes a building block for the marriage relationship. In Romans 12:6, Paul reminds us, "We have different gifts, according to the grace given us." Husbands and wives are not merely spectators in the relationship. Gifts and talents are given to enhance the marriage, as it is the church. First Corinthians 12:4 teaches us the following:

> ➢ There are diversities of gifts but the same Spirit.
> ➢ There are differences of ministries but the same Lord.
> ➢ There are diversities of activities, but it is the same God who works all in all.
> ➢ The manifestation of the Spirit is given to each one for the profit of all. First Corinthians 12:8 speaks of wisdom and knowledge, which I think is a missing link in many marriages.
> ➢ Sincerely get involved in the fellowship of believers.
> ➢ Get to know the other people in your group.
> ➢ Socialize and interact with people outside of your circle.
> ➢ Be loyal to your church
> ➢ Be committed to ministry
> ➢ Be committed to your spouse

Something is radically wrong when you look at the divorce and separation rate. Too many undeveloped babies are entering into marriage without proper instruction and guidance, just to have sex legally. Shamefully, "over 43 percent of first-time marriage end in separation or divorce" (CDC).

> Therefore, my beloved brethren, be ye steadfast, unmovable, always abounding in the work of the Lord, forasmuch as ye know that your labor is not in vain in the Lord. (1 Corinthians 15:58 KJV)

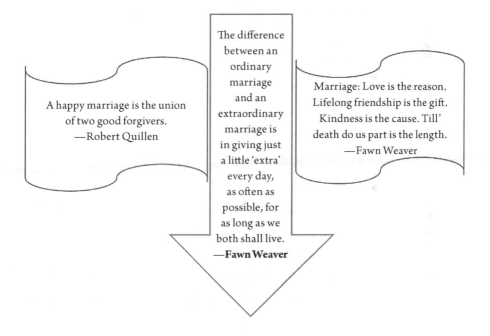

The difference between an ordinary marriage and an extraordinary marriage is in giving just a little 'extra' every day, as often as possible, for as long as we both shall live.
—Fawn Weaver

A happy marriage is the union of two good forgivers.
—Robert Quillen

Marriage: Love is the reason. Lifelong friendship is the gift. Kindness is the cause. Till' death do us part is the length.
—Fawn Weaver

Commitment is the cornerstone of creative change!

Be real. The quality of a person's life is in direct proportion to his or her commitment to excellence.

➢ There are those who think about achieving greatness; there are those who don't care.
➢ There are those who are interested in working hard; there are those who aren't interested.

- ➢ There are those who plan; there are those who don't plan.
- ➢ There are those who dream and act on their dreams; there are those who only talk about their dreams.
- ➢ There are those who are negative and criticize everything; there are those who use every negative as a positive.
- ➢ There are those who look forward; there are those who always look backward.
- ➢ There are those who look upward; there are those who always look downward.
- ➢ There are those who wish, watch, and act; there are those who only observe.
- ➢ There are those who use failure as an opportunity; there are those who just give up.
- ➢ There are those who run on the decisions of others; there are those who are totally committed to getting things done and will demonstrate their commitment with positive thoughts and actions, even if they have to do it alone.

God has placed various gifts in each of us to serve each other. If we do not do our part, we limit God in doing what he wants to do in us. God is waiting on us to act, so He can distribute to each individually as he wills. If you think, dream, plan. and act, you can make things happen.

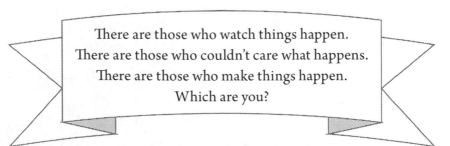

There are those who watch things happen.
There are those who couldn't care what happens.
There are those who make things happen.
Which are you?

We are all created to make things happen. That was what God told Adam in Genesis 1:26. The Lord says,

1. Stay in my presence.
2. Work.
3. Dominate everything.
4. Take responsibility.
5. Be accountable.
6. Do what is right.
7. There will be consequences if you go back on our agreement.

Our ignorance is getting more costly every day.

More than three in ten children grow up in broken homes. According to the *Richmond* [Virginia] *Times-Dispatch*, children from broken homes account for the following:

➤ 70 percent of those in juvenile detention
➤ 57 percent of all prison inmates
➤ 63 percent of teen suicide

CHAPTER 10

Learn your Spouse

Compatibility and Incompatibility

WOMEN STRETCH THEIR THOUGHTS INTO yesterday, today, and tomorrow, while men think mostly of today. Humans are very complex, and when two complex minds try to work together without knowing their areas of compatibility and incompatibility, the definitely will short-circuit because they will connect the wrong wires every time. I believe understanding is the key foundation for good communication.

If you are an English-speaking person, you cannot effectively communicate with someone speaking Chinese before you understand the language. Consequently, when two single individuals (male and female) decide to become a couple and live together for the rest of their lives, it is like learning a second language—and learning another language is never easy. It takes time to learn about someone who is your opposite.

Understanding the person's temperament is only the start. This individual could be the victim of many circumstances of which you know nothing. You may also be in the dark about the depth of any damage that he or she suffered in the past.

The Spirit of Error

Many people do not believe in dating because in their minds, dating means sexual involvement. In my own life, although we have been together for more than five decades, my wife and I faced many struggles in our relationship because we were not given proper counsel. We were not allowed to date and to get a chance to know a few things about each other. It is a new day; a time of opportunity to learn and grow.

Our Thinking vs. God's Thinking

We are hurt by what we tell ourselves,
not mainly by what people do to us.

Our Words	God's Words
It's impossible.	"All things are possible" (Luke 18:27).
I'm too tired.	"I will give you rest" (Matthew 11:28).
Nobody loves me.	"I love you" (John 3:16).
Nobody cares for me.	"He cares for you" (1 Peter 5:7).
I can't go on.	"My grace is sufficient" (2 Corinthians 12:9).
I can't figure things out.	"I will direct your paths" (Proverbs 20:24).
I can't do it.	"I can do all things" (Philippians 4:13).
I'm not able.	"I am able" (2 Corinthians 9:8).
It's not worth it.	"It will be worth it" (Romans 8:28).
I can't forgive myself.	"I will forgive you" (Psalm 103:1–2; 1 John1:9).
I can't afford it.	"I will supply all of your needs" (Philippians 4:19).

The one who walks with God will never be alone.

Save sex for marriage.

> For this is the will of God, even your sanctification, that ye should abstain from fornication. (1 Thessalonians 4:3)

> Then Amnon hated her exceedingly; so that the hatred wherewith he hated her was greater than the love wherewith he had loved her. And Amnon said unto her, Arise, be gone. And she said unto him, there is no cause: this evil in sending me away is greater than the other that thou didst unto me. But he would not hearken unto her. (2 Samuel 13:15–16)

The Dangers of Sex before Marriage

1. Loss of fellowship
2. Pregnancy
3. Abortion
4. Hate
5. Bitterness
6. Resentment
7. Anger
8. Loss of self-worth
9. Blame
10. Permanent emotional scars
11. Disrespect

CHAPTER 11

God Allows Us to Make Our Own Choices

WE ARE FREE TO DO whatever we want. God will not interfere by twisting our arms to do what is right.

A door opens and shuts. It gives entry at any time. Not so with a wall; it is solid and does not allow access.

Are you a wall or a door?

In the book of Solomon 8:8, we see the Shulamite woman recalling her youth. Her father had died when she was young, and her brothers were in charge and looked after her. Listen to the language of the brothers: "If she is a wall ..." In other words, her brothers were saying, "If our sister does not get involved in premarital sex, when men try to violate her morals, we will honor her with palace silver."

If she is a *door* (promiscuous)—meaning if she easily yields herself to men and become sexually involved by allowing them to open her *door*, then the brothers would restrict her freedom.

We are free to do whatever we want. God will not twist our arms to do what is right.

As a *door*, you will lose your peace. Someone always will be knocking.

> Dearly beloved, I beseech you as strangers and pilgrims, abstain from fleshly lusts, which war against the soul. (1 Peter 2:11

War is the absence of peace. This fleshly war keeps your life in disarray. When you yield to your flesh, there is no peace, only guilt, shame, uneasiness, and unhappiness. According to Solomon, if you commit adultery, you are senseless.

> But whoso committed adultery with a woman locket understanding he that doeth it destroyed his own soul. (Proverbs 6:32)

As a *door*, you damage your relationship with God, and it affects your character.

> Your iniquities separate you from God. He hides his face, closes his ears. (Isaiah 59:2)

Sexual sin robs your desire for spiritual things, such as prayer, reading the Word, and fellowship with God's people.

If you're a door, God cannot use you because he "cannot use a dirty vessel" (1 Timothy 2:21).

Why Are Morals Important?

Morals are important because they help guide our lives. They are the basis of what is right and wrong. They dictate how we should act in every situation and how we make decisions.

Without morals, people would be lost as to what to do or whether they were acting correctly.

> So far, about morals, I know only that what is moral is what you feel good after and what is immoral is what you feel bad after.
> —Ernest Hemingway

CHAPTER 12

Divorce and Remarriage

IN THE LAW BOOK OF heaven, when a man and a woman get married in God's divine will, and they sign a marriage document, they become joint property. It means that both are giving total rights to all that concerns them. They have entered a covenant with each other, and they have the right to make decisions together. Each is bound to the other; therefore, the covenant of marriage should be upheld in their lives, and divorce should not be an option.

> Wherefore they are no more twain, but one flesh. What therefore God hath joined together, let not man put asunder (Matthew 19:6)

Under a covenant there is 100 percent God involvement. A marriage that is sealed in heaven has God's full endorsement and can survive any storm.

In heaven's law book, it's one marriage per person. Does God keep changing his records when divorce happens?

***

The following might be somewhat controversial; it is my *personal belief* regarding earthly law and marriage. Because God gave us a free will, there is nothing he will do when decisions are made out of his will. A document of marriage can be legal on earth but not legal in heaven. Earthly actions under contract use the name of God but don't want God's interference in their lives.

***

Where God is powerless, the devil is powerful.

When an earthly marriage becomes rocky, and divorce takes place, by earthly law it is a divorce on earth. By heavenly law it is not a divorce because it was not recorded in the law book of heaven. Either party can choose to remarry by earthly law. If both parties have accepted Christ and seek God's will for their lives, God does not hold them as divorcees because the first marriage was under contract and not under heavenly covenant.

If you were married before accepting the Lord, and one party gets saved, should you just walk away?

This is a thought-provoking question, but let's look at scripture. Please note that *I am not supporting divorce* in any way. I am simply trying to give clarity to the importance of involving God in your choices.

If You Were Married as an Unsaved

> For the unbelieving husband has been sanctified through his wife, and the unbelieving wife has been sanctified through her husband. Otherwise, your children would be unclean, but as it is, they are holy. (1 Corinthians 7:14)

> But if the unbelieving wife or husband leaves, he or she is not under bondage, meaning that he or she can marry again without any heavenly penalty. (1 Corinthians 7:15)

> And he answered and said unto them, have ye not read, that he which made them at the beginning made them male and female, and said, for this cause shall a man leave father and mother, and shall cleave to his wife: and they twain shall be one flesh. (Matthew 19:4)

You don't have to walk out of your marriage because you have accepted the Lord. If the relationship becomes abusive, however, and there is constant cheating and dishonesty, after you have exhausted all your options and there is no change, it's time to pack your bags. Sin can take something as beautiful as marriage and turn it into the total opposite.

Marriage was and is a covenant between a man and a woman, with God at the head. It is important to seek God's will for your lives before entering into marriage. If you don't, you sign a contract with the devil and give him access to your lives, of which he is at the head. He will say to God, "This one belongs to me because he or she doesn't listen to you. He or she lies, steals, commits adultery, fornicates, or takes bribes. He or she is corrupt, so I have the right to do whatever I want because this person has chosen to make decisions without you and to follow me."

The devil does not want you to be under covenant with God in marriage. He wants you to be under the covenant of sin with him.

Think for a moment. What does God mean in the following scripture?

> Seek ye first the Kingdom of God, and all things
> shall be granted unto you. (Matthew 6:33)

This includes heavenly covering over your marriage.

The only way to fix a sinful marriage is to repent of your sins and denounce Satan. Break the covenant of sin with him, and allow God back into your lives. By doing that, the devil can no longer accuse you in the heavenly realms because Jesus becomes your attorney.

> Anyone who believes in him will never be put to
> shame. (Romans 10:11)

This means that when your case is presented, you will not be ashamed. Weaken Satan's power over your marriage.

> Can two walk together unless they are in
> agreement? (Amos 3:3)

It is against God's character that his children yoke themselves with unrighteousness (2 Corinthians 6:14). I strongly suggest that Christians marry Christians. I am aware of the deficiency of Christian men in the kingdom, and women allow the anxiety of companionship to dictate their futures. This is one of the reasons that Jesus encouraged evangelism and outreach in the church. Satan is holding some good men captive. There are two powerful forces in the world—Satan rules the force of darkness, but God is the force of light. These two have nothing in common. These two are not compatible.

"We are the temple of the living God" (2 Corinthians 6:16) means we are yoked to him in a binding relationship, so to be yoked with the force of darkness means we will have to unyoke with God because a yoke is meant to hold two together.

A yoke is a pair of balances that must be the same weight on two oxen. The scripture says that we should not enter into a compromising arrangement with nonbelievers (Psalm 106:28). Israel yoked themselves to Baal (Psalm 106:29). They provoked God to anger.

Christians who marry non-Christians will always experience interference from their father-in-law, the devil.

CHAPTER 13

Important Points to Ponder

THE MOST BASIC FOUNDATION OF each and every relationship should include the following:

- Have passionate love for Christ.
- Always expect the best of your relationship after doing your best.
- Base your relationship on total commitment, not just love. Love alone will not stand up during a storm, but commitment will.
- Your relationship should be a mirror of the best that God wants for your life.
- Give no place to the devil. He wants to destroy your union. He waits for the least opportunity to destroy it.
- Be sensitive to the difference the of men and women.
- Be sensitive to the differences in human nature.
- Equip yourself with knowledge to deal with differences.
- Prepare yourself to deal with the resistance to change.
- The relationship language cannot be learned overnight. Patience must be your password to success.
- Never ask for too little, and never ask for too much.
- Time is the greatest teacher. Be willing to learn from it.

- Love your spouse.
- Be committed to your spouse.
- Know and understand your spouse.
- Keep yourself attractive, inside and out.
- Have a good sense of humor.
- Trust, and allow yourself to be trusted.
- Master pride and anger.
- Maintain your integrity in every area.
- Lest you respond in an offensive tone, take a long, deep breath, then slowly let it out. Talk less; listen more.
- Be each other's best friend.
- Change your *I* or *me* to *we* or *us*. Avoid pointing the finger!

CHAPTER 14

Do You Know Who You Are?

WHEN INDIVIDUALS DISCOVER THEIR OWN basic temperaments, they can easily figure out what vocational opportunities they should pursue, how to get along with other people, what natural weaknesses to watch for, what type of spouses they should marry, and how they can improve the effectiveness of their lives (LaHaye 1991). Each temperament has its own set of responses to life. Therefore, it is expected that each temperament will react in different ways (Rust 1977).

Let's look at the following temperaments and the expected reactions, using negatives and positives.

Melancholic

Negative Tendencies

Those with a *melancholic* temperament are aloof, withdrawn, suffer from low self-esteem, sometime do not like themselves, develop self-destructive feelings, and set unreachable standards.

If violated, they find it very hard to trust again. If abused, melancholics will end up hating themselves and see themselves as unintelligent or not good enough.

If they perceive that they will be rejected, they first reject others. Consequently, they suffer from depression, stress, fear, low self-esteem, and moodiness. Moreover, they can become uncomfortable in large groups and sometimes find it hard to engage in conversation because they do not like to sound foolish, so they prefer to be silent.

Positive Tendencies

Melancholics are thinkers and possess high intellectual abilities. They are very private and reserved. They can easily see pitfalls and have good decision-making abilities. They are emotionally guarded, task-oriented, self-motivated, well-organized, and like to be sure about a project before getting involved. Furthermore, they like to see everything in black and white. They are trustworthy, orderly, possess good leadership abilities, and understand tasks and systems. They are loyal and self-sacrificing and are faithful friends and great teachers. The world could never do without the melancholics.

Supine

This temperament was developed by Drs. Richard and Phyllis Arno of the National Christian Counselor Association.

Negative Tendencies

Those with a supine temperament are natural-born victims. Their lives are filled with anxiety and anger. They find it difficult to stand up against authority because they are always looking for a father or mother image. If their trust is betrayed and they are pushed beyond limits, their bottled-up anger will cause them to act like the melancholic by turning their anger inside and letting it brew until they explode like an erupting volcano. Eventually, they will seek to hurt those who betrayed them. Supines need validation and approval.

Positive Tendencies

Supines have a gentle spirit and a servant's heart. They are trusting, teachable, and respond easily to love. Supines are very dependable. They are relationship-oriented, very loving and caring, and express great strengths. Additionally, they are introverted and extroverted, with the ability to undertake numerous tasks and the need to relate to people. Their teachable spirit makes them good followers who enforce polices set by others.

Sanguine

Negative Tendencies

Those with a sanguine temperament display histrionic behaviors. They are identified in a crowd by their neurotic need for attention and social approval. Sanguines are the pendulum type. They exaggerate and are weak-willed. They adapt easily to bad morals with a tendency to repeat the mistakes of yesterday. Sanguines are people-driven; they need constant affirmations that they are loved and appreciated.

Positive Tendencies

Sanguines are friendly, warm, enthusiastic, optimistic, and charming. They interact well with others. They like people and are caring. They express and receive much love and affection. They are warm, relationship-oriented, outgoing, and inspiring.

Choleric

Negative Tendencies

Those with a choleric temperament are hot-tempered, cruel, and angry. They appear charming and friendly but with the motive of self-gratification. They are domineering and think no one should reject their manipulation for love and affection.

Positive Tendencies

Cholerics are confident, optimistic, and tough-minded. They are great leaders and take on responsibilities to get the job done. They are very selective in deep relationships.

Phlegmatic

Negative Tendencies

Those with a phlegmatic temperament tend to be observers. They raise verbal defenses and have a tendency to remain uninvolved. They usually procrastinate and are unmotivated, unemotional, slow, and stubborn.

Positive Tendencies

Phlegmatics are calm, cool, easygoing, and peaceful. They are not easily shaken by anything. They are not demanding. They always play the arbitrator and spend time making sure the job is well done.

> For you created my inmost being and you knit me together in my mother's womb. I praise you because I am fearfully and wonderfully made; your works are wonderful; I know that full well. My frame was not hidden from you when I was made in the secret place. When I was woven together in the depths of the earth, your eyes saw my unformed body. All the days ordained for me were written in your book before one of them came to be. (Psalm 139:13–16)

Through divine inspiration, David knew that before he was born, God designed him. While our bodies were being differentiated within our mothers' wombs, each inward part was designed exactly as God intended—including both our strengths and our weaknesses.

CHAPTER 15

The Road to Marriage and Beyond

The Foundation of Friendship

BECAUSE DATING IS BASED ON friendship, if individuals develop a sound friendship, they will develop a good dating relationship.

Who is a friend? A friend is someone on whom you can call at any time, and he or she will be there without judging you. A friend is someone you can visit without advance notice. A friend is someone with whom you can share a secret and know it will be safe. A friend will stand with you under pressure, regardless of the cause.

Never rush a friendship. In most cases, it is a slow growing process. There can be, however, a sudden bond that just happens. Opposite temperaments can draw two people together, resulting in a lasting friendship.

Neither you nor your friend should be cheap.

A sound friendship will possess the following characteristics:

❖ Together, you laugh, cry, and share deep inner feelings.
❖ You have a willingness to sacrifice for the other person.

❖ Absence leaves you with an inner emptiness.
❖ If your friend succeeds in a venture, you are genuinely happy.
❖ You always find it easy to overlook each other's faults.
❖ You can always confide without fear of betrayal.
❖ Communication is free and comfortable.

Choose your friends carefully. Nevertheless, "Be not unequally yoked with unbelievers" (2 Corinthians 6:14).

Real friends don't always agree on everything, but even during disagreements, they will make every effort to preserve the friendship. Deep friendship requires commitment, a base on which to stand.

> The light of friendship is like the light of phosphorus, seen plainest when all around is dark.
>
> —Grace Crowell

Dating

Dating must be looked at in the context of an opposite-sex relationship

Casual Dating

Casual dating is devoid of special emotional involvement with the other person. It could involve someone you do not even like very much, but you are dating merely to alleviate boredom, or you may just need companionship for a short while.

Casual dating only should serve to pass time. This is when one party may have a one-sided love but cannot express it because of fear of losing the opportunity of a second chance

Sometimes doing small things are messages, but the other party simply says thank you with no type of emotion. The individual might view the other simply as a nice person. There is no holding of hands. No personal matters are discussed, just superficial conversations.

Sometimes the little fires of casual dating eventually become a forest fire that leads to special dating.

Special Dating

When you are invited out on this date, just the sound of the person's voice makes you feel a tingle and causes goose bumps on your skin. You can hardly wait for the date so you can spend time with this person. You keep checking your closet, thinking of what to wear, because you are conscious of how you will look. Women think of what makeup they will use. They practice their walks and all the things that will make a good impression.

Men think of getting a haircut, finding the right shirt, shining their shoes, and practicing their speech. The man thinks of how he will hurriedly get out to open her car door. Everything seems very important at that time because a good impression matters. He thinks of the old saying, "The first impression is a lasting one."

Steady Dating

Steady dating has a commitment. You will not turn down this person for any other. There is a certain chemistry, which causes you to feel totally committed and confident. The man probably carries an engagement ring in his pocket. The woman's mind is set on alert, looking and listening for the next move or the next question. Pretending not to look, she sees him reach into his pocket and put his hand behind him. He says, "I've been waiting for the right moment to do this." He sets her on edge by saying, "I've never done this before, so I'm trying to get it right. I don't know what you are going to say. Oh, I am probably making a fool of myself. This is not easy. OK. Will you marry me?"

Engagement

Engagement comes after dating but before marriage. In other words, engagement is the preparatory period leading up to marriage. Engagement is not marriage, and so it is important for the couple to conduct a clean life without becoming sexually intimate during that time.

Dating also should be clean.

Warning: Even with an engagement ring on her finger, some never make it to marriage because of mistakes made during the engagement.

Many books have been written on the subject of dating, but some do not embrace morals. I feel that colleges and high schools could play a vital role in the lives of young people by encouraging them to embrace good morals. Most of the confusion today stems from what is taught in classrooms and books. How can we know a lie from the truth or right from wrong? The Bible is more than a good book. It is the guidebook and road map that will guide you safely to your destination.

The Bible is God speaking.

> Every Scripture is God breathed (given by His inspiration) and profitable for instruction, for reproof and conviction of sin, for correction of error and discipline in obedience, (and) for training in righteousness (in holy living, in conformity to God's will in thought purpose, and action), so that the man of God may be complete and proficient, well fitted and thoroughly equipped for every good work. (2 Timothy 3:16–17 AMP)

Marriage

Marriage is one of God's greatest gifts to humans. Sadly, many people enter marriage based on emotions, which will not survive a little wind. For a marriage to survive storms, it must be based on commitment, not love. God designed the institution of marriage to be honorable, and it should not be entered into ignorantly but with proper guidance.

When a man and woman have sought guidance from the Lord during the dating period and have preserved themselves from sexual temptations, they can truly say they have weathered the sexual storms of dating, saving the best wine for last. They present themselves as two people who can proudly look each other in the eye without feeling ashamed or guilty because of sexual violation. This brings joy to the heart of God.

I know it is hard to enter a marriage based on faith, but it is right. You may not be a virgin at the time of marriage because of past mistakes, but if you start this relationship right, it will last. God will honor your faith because you have performed a sexual fast to honor him.

Marriage is full of excitement and fun. The sexual attractions, romance, and passion are elements to be desired, but there will be times when other areas take precedence.

I must warn you of some mistakes that will affect your marriage. Traditionally, the bride dresses in a beautiful gown, maybe with a long train; she has bridesmaids and flower girls. The groom wears a tuxedo, and the groomsmen all are nicely matched. Many brides say they want their weddings to be big and exciting. There are long hours of planning. Much effort, strength, energy, and money are usually spent for the occasion.

The mistake many make is in putting more into the wedding than the marriage. It is best to keep your wedding day simple, and make your marriage great.

Some marriages suffer because too much money was spent for the wedding. Three months down the road, the white gown and tux are hanging in the closet. Some gifts are still unopened. There is leftover cake in the freezer, but the couple has begun to experience financial problems, and all the bliss, fun, joy, and laughter of the wedding day slowly is sliding away.

I believe couples deserve to have a good time, but if you cannot afford a big wedding, it is OK. What matters most is the marriage, not the wedding.

> Never overspend; you will crash.
> It is always better to keep it
> simple and live happily.

Postmarriage Dating

Most people date before marriage because it is the getting-to-know-you period. Everyone likes to make a good impression on the person with whom he or she is hoping to share the future. Still, it is mind-boggling when you hear the stories of the premarriage era of relationships—the fun, laughter, good companionship, and the sweet memories of times spent together.

Unfortunately, after a few short months or years of marriage, couples are caught in various circumstance-driven situations. Problems such as money, sex, illness, family members, and a vast array of other issues have caused couples to lose the sizzle in their marriage relationship. They drift slowly apart from each other.

When this happens, dating becomes a thing of the past.

Dating should be practiced during marriage. It should continue even more than before marriage. This will kindle the flames and keep your marriage fresh, even after many years together. Proper maintenance of the relationship will prevent it from rusting or wearing away.

Marriage is a covenant between two people (male and female). There are benefits to keeping it and penalties for breaking it. The foundation of the relationship is friendship that brings two people together in oneness. The marriage relationship is compared to relationship with God. His words are unchanging and steadfast. God desires commitment in marriage, just as he is committed to us.

CHAPTER 16

Trust Is Built; Commitment Is a Choice

TRUST IS A KEY FACTOR in relationships. It takes a lifetime to build but can be broken in a moment.

Webster's Revised Unabridged Dictionary defines trust as follows:

1. Assured resting of the mind on the integrity, veracity, justice, friendship, or other sound principle, of another person; confidence; reliance.

2. To place confidence in; to rely on, to confide, or repose faith in; as, we cannot trust those who have deceived us.

3. To give credence to; to believe; to credit

Trust is like a vase—once it's broken, though you can fix it, the vase will never be same again.
—Walter Anderson

> ➤ Trust is the glue of life. It's the most essential ingredient in effective commitment.
> ➤ Trust is the easiest thing in the world to lose and the hardest thing to build.
> ➤ Trust broken will suddenly change the trajectory of anything, regardless of its former strength.

Trust, honesty, humility, transparency, and accountability are the building blocks of a strong relationship. If trust is removed, the entire foundation is weakened, and all the other blocks lose their effectiveness. The sacrifices, effort, good intentions, and hard work become incapable of producing any useful result.

> ➤ Trust is built on truth, not on telling someone what he or she wants to hear. Trust starts and ends with truth.
> ➤ Trust is consistent; it does not waver.
> ➤ Trust eliminates fear.
> ➤ Trust creates possibilities.
> ➤ Trust makes love real.

Successful relationships are built on *trust* and *truth*.

Trust

Transparency: Have no hidden agenda.
Reliability: Your word is your bond.
Understanding: This makes it easier to trust.
Sacrifice and sincerity: Nothing is too hard.
Teamwork: Together, you will accomplish a task.

Truth

Treat others with respect/
Responsibility is necessary for every action.
Unity means standing together.
Trust begets trust
Honesty—no one succeeds without it.

Relationships

Require trust
Encouragement
Long-lasting love
Always patient
Truthfulness
Interest
Oneness
Natural approach
Sowing into each other
Humbleness of heart
Invest in each other
Put the other person first

Trust, as it is used in the Bible, means to have confidence in, place reliance upon, expect, believe, and entrust. We are to trust in God and his love to guide our lives, both in this reality and the next. The Bible warns us not to place trust in our money, job, possessions, ourselves, or others. Trust is the common denominator in every area of life:

➤ Relationships

- ➤ Spiritual life
- ➤ Teams
- ➤ Business
- ➤ Organizations
- ➤ Government

People often say, "Trust me." The truth is that if there is real trust within you, it will manifest without your having to convince someone to do so.

- ➤ We were not born with trust; it must be built.
- ➤ Trust knows when it has been violated.
- ➤ Trust has its own voice. You cannot bargain with it. You can rebuild it, but it may never be the same.

Developed trust has the potential to create unparalleled success in relationships.

- ➤ Trust impacts us with every tick of the clock, yet it is often treated lightly.
- ➤ Trust is what keeps you glowing through difficult times.
- ➤ Trust undergirds relationships.
- ➤ Trust enhances communication.
- ➤ Trust produces positive results in family, work, and every area of life.
- ➤ Trust is pragmatic; it deals with things practical rather than theoretical, not what it could or should be.
- ➤ Trust is not illusive; it is based on something real.
- ➤ Trust is the base of commitment. You can only commit to a relationship after you've built the trust foundation.
- ➤ Trust erases fear in the mind of the other person.

No one will honestly commit to a relationship they don't trust. Believers commit to following God because of their trust in him. Trust affects every human on the planet. I've often heard clients say, "I've been burned so much in the past. I just can't trust anyone anymore."

My first response to that person is one simple question: "Does that include you?" Stop and think for a moment—if you kill trust, you are killing yourself without a weapon, and you will become a walking corpse.

Do you stop eating because you do not trust the food at two or three restaurants? If you decide to grow your own food, do you trust the seeds you purchase? You will have to trust somebody or something. You just can't live without trust, so get hold of yourself.

Trust is like a coin; it has two sides—your side and the other person's side. There is low trust and high trust.

You may have a high level of trust in your spouse Then something happens that causes high trust to fall, uncertainty creeps in, and now it becomes low trust that leads to no trust. This is when you examine the coin. What or who caused this? In many cases, the blame is unfairly passed on to the other person. Read Matthew 7:3–5 about the speck and the plank.

> The moment there is a suspicion about a person's motive, everything he does becomes tainted.
> —Mahatma Gandhi

CHAPTER 17

Questions to Ask Before (or After) You Say "I Do"

IF YOU ARE PREPARING FOR marriage or experiencing marital conflict, carefully look through and answer the following questions. They will help you to make wise decisions.

Some of the questions appear in the form of what-if scenarios. In most cases, the answers are idealistic because persons are not experiencing the emotions involved at that time. Answering the questions honestly will be to your benefit.

Check the questions as they apply to you.

1. You are having an intense emotional conflict with your spouse. You are extremely tired, and it's getting very late. How do you feel about going to bed without a resolution?
    [] OK to go to bed
    [] Not OK

2. Check as many boxes as apply to you:
    This is a picture of my social life:
    [] I like to have several friends.

[] I like parties and social gatherings/activities.
[] I prefer family gatherings.
[] I don't need a lot of people.
[] All I need is one good friend.
[] I see enough people at work.
[] People give me energy.
[] People drain my energy.

3. Are you comfortable with the communication level between you and your partner?
   {} Yes
   {} No
   {} Sometimes
   {} I wish we were able to share more.
   {} I am not the talkative type.

4. Does your partner share his or her feelings and thoughts as much as you'd like?
   {} I wish my partner would share more.
   {} Yes, for the most part.
   {} We rarely express our feelings.

5. Ideally, I would prefer to:
   [] Live in a big city (many activities)
   [] Live in a small city (not many activities)
   [] Live in a small town where there are not many people
   [] Live on a lake
   [] Don't care as long as we can get back and forth
   [] Not sure what I want

6. Do you or your partner find yourselves often using the words *always* and *never*?
    [ ] I do.
    [ ] My partner does.
    [ ] Neither of us does.

7. When something is bothering me, I tend to
    [ ] remain quiet.
    [ ] hope that my partner will notice and pry it out of me.
    [ ] talk about it until I feel better.
    [ ] deal with it my way, on my terms.

8. If something is bothering your partner, do you think he or she would talk to you freely about it?
    [ ] Yes
    [ ] Maybe not immediately, but eventually
    [ ] Not sure

9. Does your partner maintain eye contact, give feedback to let you know he or she is listening, and allow you to finish your thoughts without interrupting?
    [ ] Yes
    [ ] No
    [ ] Not as much as I'd like

10. Does he or she allow you to have your own opinion without trying to get his or her point across?
    [ ] Yes, most of the time
    [ ] Sometimes
    [ ] No

11. In some disagreements where a compromise is not an option, who wins?
[] The one who feels strongest on the subject
[] Me
[] My spouse
[] We flip a coin
[] Neither; we try to find some humor in it

12. Operating an automobile sometimes says a lot about who we really are. What are some of your partner's habits?
[] Opens the door for you
[] Locks the doors, has keen awareness and cautiousness
[] Wears seatbelt always
[] Wears seatbelt only when the police are spotted
[] Drives too fast
[] Inattentive and reckless
[] Drives too reckless when upset
[] Overconfident
[] Very cautious
[] Just average

13. Who has a higher need for verbal expression?
[] Me
[] My partner
[] We agree equally

14. Your spouse tells you that you are not spending enough time with the family. How would the question be posed?
[] You are not spending any time with this family, and you need to.

[ ] I wish we could spend more time together as a family.

15. Where do you stand regarding modesty around family members?
    [ ] I do what makes me comfortable.
    [ ] Walking around in underwear is no big deal.
    [ ] Although they are family members, I should be fully clothed around them.
    [ ] The children can be allowed to go without diapers and climb and sit on the lap of their family members and visitors.

16. What if your spouse embarrassed you in a humorous comment in the presence of others? You would:
    [ ] Be embarrassed but say nothing
    [ ] Counter with a joke about your spouse
    [ ] Ask your spouse to stop because it's hurtful
    [ ] Laugh at the moment but explode at home

17. How do you feel when you make a mistake?
    [ ] I try to learn from it.
    [ ] I beat up on myself for days.
    [ ] I tend to blame someone or something; it makes me feel better.
    [ ] I admit it and try not to repeat it.

18. How do you generally react to change?
    [ ] Quite easily.
    [ ] I don't like change; life is already complicated.

19. My partner is:
    [ ] Easy to get along with

[] Somewhat uptight, irritate

20. When there's a disagreement, do the words *you* and *your* come up quite often?
    [] Never.
    [] Sometimes.
    [] Not often.
    [] We do not argue.

21. I see myself as:
    [] Easy to get along with
    [] Sometime a little uptight

22. What if your partner threatens to discontinue the relationship because of something you refuse to change?
    [] I do everything I can to change.
    [] I end the relationship. I don't take kindly to an ultimatum.
    [] I only try to change if it was something I don't like about myself.

23. When my partner is going through difficult times, I do the following:
    [] Try to be consoling
    [] Would rather not be around him or her
    [] Assume it has something to do with me

24. Does your partner drink strong drinks?
    [] No.
    [] Yes, sometime the amount bothers me.
    [] Yes, he or she acts differently after drinking.

25. When I am not physically well, I:
    [] Like to be left alone
    [] Try to act as though all is well
    [] Moan and groan more than I should
    [] Feel bad that I am not able to do what I need to do

26. When I'm in a bad mood, I:
    [] Tend to say things I don't mean
    [] Tend to raise my voice
    [] Find someone to talk to until I feel better
    [] Talk sarcastically
    [] Go shopping
    [] Still maintain respect to those around me

Every couple will encounter certain issues during the marriage: money, sex, family, children, job situations, household chores, church involvement, likes and dislikes, and other issues. To what extent have you addressed these issues?

Circle one of the following answers to each question.

To the best of your knowledge:

1. Does your partner always tell the truth? Yes No Not sure
2. Is your partner honest with you? Yes No Not sure
3. Do you like each other's friends? Yes No Not sure
4. Are you suspicious of your partner? Yes No Not sure
5. Is you partner quick to forgive? Yes No Not sure
6. Does your partner have a good sense of humor? Yes No Not sure

7. Do you think you will be able to meet each other's sexual needs? Yes No Not sure

8. Do you feel the same way about treating each other fairly? Yes No Not sure

9. Does your partner have abusive tendencies? Yes No Not sure

10. Does either of you have a problem communicating? Yes No Sometimes

11. Do you like the way your partner looks, smells, and dresses? Yes No Not sure

12. Would you both choose to live in the same locale? Yes No Not sure

13. Do you respect each other's political and religious views? Yes No Sometimes

14. Will you feel relaxed and sexually uninhibited with your partner? Yes No Not sure

15. Will you be able to express affection in nonsexual ways, such as cuddling, gifts, kissing, playing? Yes No Not sure

16. Would you trust him or her with your life? Yes No Not sure

17. Is he or she afraid to talk openly about lovemaking? Yes No Not sure

18. Is he or she your best friend? Yes No Not sure

19. Would you rather spend time with him or her than with anyone else? Yes No Not sure

20. When a problem arises, do you trust that you can go to your partner first for help? Yes No Not sure

21. Does your partner have anger issues that places doubts in your mind? Yes No Not sure

22. Do you have trouble with anger issues? Yes No Sometimes

23. Will you allow each other to make mistakes? Yes No Not sure

24. Does your partner admit when he or she is wrong? Yes No Not sure

25. Do you respect each other's opinion and viewpoint (generally)? Yes No Not sure

26. Will you be able to take vacations together? Yes No Not sure

27. Does your partner respect your intelligence? Yes No Not sure

28. If you have different viewpoints, can you agree to disagree? Yes No Not sure

29. Do you look forward to your partner coming home when he or she is out? Yes No Not sure

Avoidance of the following issues by refusing to discuss them could lead to major problems in marriage. Do any of the following apply to you?

1. Abortion: Would you ever agree to an abortion? Have you ever had an abortion?

2. Children: Do you presently have a child or children?

3. Divorce: Have you ever been divorced?

4. Bisexuality: Are you sexually attracted by both men and women?

5. Homosexuality: Do you have tendencies or feelings for the same sex?

6. Pregnancy: Are you pregnant now? If so, how will it affect your marriage?

7. How long have you known each other?
8. How long have you been in this relationship?
9. How well do you handle constructive criticism?
10. What do you like most about him/her?
    Explain what you dislike about your partner.
11. In what ways are both of you alike or different?
12. Are you easily offended? Yes No Sometimes
    If yes, in what way?
13. Why do you want to get married to him or her and not to someone else?
14. Do you know the difference between love and infatuation? Explain your answer.
15. How would you define love?
16. Do you genuinely love this person?
17. What is the worst thing that you could discover about your partner and still love him or her?
18. Do you have a stable occupation? Yes No
19. Describe what you do for a living.
20. Do you like your job?
21. Do your parents approve or disapprove of your choice for marriage?
    Explain your answer
22. Do you relate well to your mother, father, and/or guardian? Explain your relationship.
23. Will you invite them to your wedding?
    Explain your answer.
    If your parents are separated or divorced, how has it affected you?
24. Describe briefly any recent conflict with your partner and how it was handled.

25. Were you in a previous relationship? If yes, how did it end?

   How soon after the breakup did you enter into this relationship?

   Does your partner know anything about this?

   If yes, what was his or her reaction?

26. Do you plan to have children? Yes No Maybe

   Was this discussed?

27. How soon after marriage do you intend to have children?

28. What do you expect of your partner?

   How do you feel about household chores (cooking, bed-making, housecleaning, laundry, lawn, dishes, etc.)?

29. In one word, what is the most important thing that holds a marriage together?

30. Do you and your partner talk about birth control?

   If yes, have you decided on which method you will use as a couple?

   Have you read and discussed its reliability, cost, and side effects?

31. Because of what others have told you, when you think about sex, does this make you anxious?

32. Would you tell your partner if he or she satisfies you sexually?

33. Who should initiate sex: husband, wife, or both? Explain your answer.

34. What is your view of sex before marriage?

35. What type of music do you and your partner like?

36. How do you react when you are angry (raise your voice, throw things, walk out of the house, slam doors, hitting, don't talk, etc.)?

37. When there is a disagreement, do you usually discuss the issue, try to prove you are right, knuckle under, or negotiate a satisfying resolution?

38. What are your long-range goals (five years and over)?

39. 39. What are your short-range goals (under five years)?

40. 40. Do any of your relatives depend on you financially?

41. Do you have life insurance coverage for your family and/or health insurance coverage?

42. Do you plan to write your will shortly after the wedding?

43. If you are experiencing conflict as a couple, to whom would you turn?

44. Do you believe in counseling to help you to resolve personal problems?

45. How do you react when people do not see things your way?

46. 46. Do you tell your partner when he or she is right or wrong?

47. Sometimes, kind or nice people say hurtful things. How do you think you will handle contradictions like this in each other?

48. How do you think you will handle life reversals (unemployment, debt, sickness, etc.)?

49. Why are the following points important to a healthy family life?
    Appreciation of each other
    Planned time together
    Positive communication patterns
    Sensitive listening
    Do you practice these? Yes No Not sure Sometimes

50. Circle the following headings you are unsure about or dislike about your partner:

1. Hygiene
2. Physique
3. Profession
4. Eating habits
5. Sleeping habits
6. Sexual demands
7. Money handling
8. Dependence/independence
9. Mannerisms
10. Clothing styles
11. Refusal or afraid to address the topic of sex
12. Upset when the word sex is mentioned
13. Attitude toward his or her parents or family
14. Attitude toward your parents or family
15. Attitude toward children
16. Attitude toward animals
17. Attitude toward your associates
    Consistent or inconsistent
    Jealous
    Laid back

To give a brief overview of your true feelings, check the questions that apply to you.

I am marrying because:

1. ( ) I want to escape an unhappy stressful situation.
2. ( ) I want to share myself completely with my partner.
3. ( ) I want to commit myself completely to my partner.

4. ( ) I feel that marriage will let me feel less lonely.
5. ( ) Everybody keeps pressuring me to get married.
6. ( ) I feel I have gone too far with my partner, and it would be better to marry him or her.
7. ( ) I find my partner is perfect in every way.
8. ( ) I do not see any shortcomings in my partner.
9. ( ) I want to be my partner's companion for life.
10. ( ) I feel very romantic toward my partner.
11. ( ) The sexual pressure is too much for me.
12. ( ) I think I can help my partner have a better life; he or she has not been treated fairly.
13. ( ) I need help financially.
14. ( ) All my friends are married.
15. ( ) Soon I will be too old.
16. ( ) I completely trust my partner.
17. ( ) My partner would never do anything to hurt me.

If you checked more than six of the above questions, review the questions again because there are only six answers that should be answered checked. If you cannot narrow your answers to six, evaluate your thinking and ask yourself, "Why do I really want to get married?"

Roles in the Marriage

The following balance sheet is to see how both wife and husband think.

Circle a number for each question.

1. Unsure/Both

2. No/Never
3. Sometimes
4. Agree
5. Strongly agree

1. The husband should be priest, prophet, and king in the home.

   1 2 3 4 5

2. It is the wife's responsibility to do the housework.

   1 2 3 4 5

3. A wife should not work outside of the home.

   1 2 3 4 5

4. Husbands are not required to help with household chores.

   1 2 3 4 5

5. Wives should not interfere with the way a husband spends money.

   1 2 3 4 5

6. Husband and wife should plan a budget and manage money matters together.

   1 2 3 4

7. Husband and wife should avoid having joint credit cards accounts.

   1 2 3 4 5

8. Neither husband nor wife should purchase an item without the knowledge of the other.

   1 2 3 4 5

9. The husband should take his wife out at least twice a month.

   1 2 3 4 5

10. The wife is responsible for the children's discipline, not the husband.

1 2 3 4 5

11. Since they are not biological parents, neither husband nor wife should discipline children who were brought into the marriage.

1 2 3 4 5

12. It is the husband's job to go to work to support his family.

1 2 3 4 5

13. Children should not be allowed to join in the planning of family activities or vacations.

1 2 3 4 5

14. The wife's money belongs to her, even when the husband is not working.

1 2 3 4 5

15. Both wife and husband should be allowed to have their own close friends.

1 2 3 4 5

16. When problems arise in a relationship, both husband and wife should seek counseling together.

1 2 3 4 5

17. The husband's responsibility is to work outside the home.

1 2 3 4 5

18. The wife's responsibility is in the home, and she should not work outside.

1 2 3 4 5

19. Husband and wife share equal rights in the marriage.

1 2 3 4 5

20. Submission means that the wife is inferior to the husband.

1 2 3 4 5

21. Since the wife should obey her husband, if he tells her to do something, she should, even if it is illegal.

1 2 3 4 5

22. When a wife does not do everything that her husband says, she is disobedient.

1 2 3 4 5

23. Are you prepared to live with the dislikes/faults of your mate?

Yes No Maybe

24. Are you aware that you cannot change your partner, but you can change yourself?

Yes No

25. Are you willing to trust God to change your partner where change is needed?

Yes No

CHAPTER 18

Marriage Scriptures

THE LORD GOD SAID, "IT is not good for the man to be alone. I will make a helper suitable for him." The LORD God had formed out of the ground all the beasts of the field and all the birds of the air. He brought them to the man to see what he would name them; and whatever the man called each living creature, that was its name. So the man gave names to all the livestock, the birds of the air and all the beasts of the field. But for Adam no suitable helper was found.

> So the LORD God caused the man to fall into a deep sleep; and while he was sleeping, he took one of the man's ribs and closed up the place with flesh. Then the LORD God made a woman from the rib he had taken out of the man, and he brought her to the man. The man said, "This is now bone of my bones and flesh of my flesh; she shall be called 'woman, for she was taken out of man." For this reason a man will leave his father and mother and be united to his wife, and they will become one flesh. The man and his

wife were both naked, and they felt no shame.
(Genesis 2:18–25)

For the husband is the head of the wife as Christ
is the head of the church, his body, of which he is
the Savior. Now as the church submits to Christ,
so also wives should submit to their husbands in
everything. (Ephesians 5:23–24)

"For this reason a man will leave his father and
mother and be united to his wife, and the two will
become one flesh." This is a profound mystery—
but I am talking about Christ and the church.
(Ephesians 5:31–32)

Wives, submit to your husbands, as is fitting in
the Lord. Husbands, love your wives and do not
be harsh with them. (Colossians 3:18–19)

Husbands, in the same way be considerate as you live
with your wives and treat them with respect as the weaker
partner and as heirs with you of the gracious gift of life, so that
nothing will hinder your prayers. Finally, all of you, live in
harmony with one another; be sympathetic, love as brothers,
be compassionate and humble.

Do not repay evil with evil or insult with insult,
but with blessing, because to this you were called
so that you may inherit a blessing. For, Whoever
would love life and see good days must keep

his tongue from evil and his lips from deceitful speech. (1 Peter 3:7–10 NIV)

He must manage his own family well and see that his children obey him with proper respect. (If anyone does not know how to manage his own family, how can he take care of God's church?) (1 Timothy 3:4–5)

CHAPTER 19

Client's Information Form

Client's Information for Counselor or Pastor **Short Form** PLEASE PRINT or write clearly. First Name Last Name
Address City State ZIP
Home Phone Work Phone Cell Phone Email
Referred by Home church Address of church Date of wedding Name of pastor Telephone

[] Male [] Female
Race
Age

Place of birth
Mother's name
Father's name

Parents: Married [] Single [] Divorced [] Widowed []

Briefly describe your reason for seeking counseling.

CHAPTER 20

Some Main Points to Consider

1. Single life gives you time to modify your behavior.
2. Correct your thinking to be a victor, not a victim.
3. Develop yourself, and set goals.
4. Learn from others without being a copycat.
5. Be a gift to your spouse.
6. Sex is not something you use to hold on to a man.
7. Wearing revealing attire for attraction does not work for the man who is looking for a life partner.
8. You cannot be yourself until you like yourself
9. "We are created in the image of God" (Genesis 1:26). "We are children of God" (John 1:12).
10. Self-confidence is important to a successful marriage. Jesus advised us, "Love our neighbor as ourselves" (Mark 12:31).
11. The Lord wants you to love yourself.
12. Dating should be kept clean (devoid of sex).
13. Because of some of the mistakes made during the dating period, some never make it to marriage.
14. Dating is not for everyone. Some people have severe sexual weaknesses, so be careful who you date.

15. There is a difference between the wedding and the marriage.
16. Postmarriage dating should be practiced often to keep the marriage fresh.

It is through our pardon, we are pardoned
When tempted to hate, sow love
When tempted to sow despair, sow hope
When tempted to sow sadness, sow joy
When there is gross darkness, be a light
Where there is unbelief, sow faith

—author unknown

ABOUT THE AUTHOR

DR. ALBERT HIBBERT has served in various areas of church ministry and has been a pastor for over forty years. He also has worked in the corporate world in supervisory and managerial positions. He is a licensed clinical Christian counselor, psychotherapist, and cognitive therapist under the National Christian Counselor Association (NCCA) in Sarasota, Florida.

Dr. Hibbert has trained and licensed many counselors. Some are active in the counseling field today. For many years, Dr. Hibbert operated his private practice in the northern and southern United States and the Caribbean, bringing hope to the hopeless and healing to the wounded and hurting.

Credentials:

PhD in counseling, Family Bible College and Seminary, Baltimore, Maryland

MA in counseling, Cornerstone University, Lake Charles, Louisiana

BA, Calvary Theological Seminary, Lake Charles, Louisiana

NCCA licensed clinical pastoral counselor, Sarasota, Florida

Board certified, Sarasota Academy of Christian Clinical Therapists.

Trained in rational emotive behavior therapy, Albert Ellis Institute, New York.

Board certified, substance abuse and addiction therapy (NCCA)

Approved instructor, Evangelical Training Association (ETA)
Past diplomat American Psychotherapy Association (APA)

Past Memberships:

- American College of Forensic Counselors (ACFC)
- American Association of Christian Counselors (AACC)
- Georgia Christian Counselors Association (GCCA)
- National Board of Christian Clinical Therapists (NBCCT)

Dr. Hibbert has been married for over fifty years and has three sons and three grandchildren.

Printed in the United States
by Baker & Taylor Publisher Services